SPACE

Written by
Berry-Anne Billingsley

Illustrated by
Maltings Partnership, Oxford Illustrators
Mike Gilkes

Designed by
Janice English

Edited by
Lisa Hyde

Picture Research by
David Cottingham

CONTENTS

Aliens

How many stars are there?
How big is the universe?
Are there any aliens?

Suppose we are about to go on a rocket trip into outer space. It would take thousands of years to reach the nearest star in an ordinary rocket. So suppose this rocket can travel at the speed of light – the fastest speed possible.

First it must leave our planet, the Earth. The Earth's force of gravity pulls the rocket to the ground. At last we have lift-off and now the rocket is gliding freely through space.

We steer past other planets in the solar system. The Earth is one of nine planets which go around the Sun. They are spread across millions of kilometres. An ordinary rocket would take about twelve years to reach the outermost planet, Pluto. It takes just five and a half hours at the speed of light.

Now we are in outer space. It is black and empty. We see occasional wisps of dust and once we run into a storm of little rocky meteoroids. Most days we see nothing at all. We are on the way to **Proxima Centauri**, the nearest star. We finally arrive 4½ years later.

Our Sun and Proxima Centauri are two stars in a gigantic swirl of stars, called the **Milky Way**. This is our home galaxy. In the universe there are millions of galaxies and in every galaxy there are millions of stars.

Perhaps some of these other stars also have planets. Perhaps one such planet has intelligent life . . . and perhaps, one day, they will make contact.

How big is the universe?

Imagine there was an alien on the other side of the universe. How long would it take us to get there?

Do aliens really exist?

The fact is no one knows. The universe is so big that so far humans have only searched the tiniest corner of it. There will always be more to find out about space, because there will always be new places to explore.

This book tells you some of the things scientists have already found out and describes some of the mysteries they are still trying to solve.

Astronomical dictionary

Astronomer Person who watches the stars.

Star The Sun is a star – a giant ball of burning gas, 100 times bigger than the Earth. Stars make heat and light.

Solar system Some stars have planets. A planet is a ball of rock or gas which circles around a star. A star with its planets is called a **solar system**.

Galaxy Stars group together in huge swirls called **galaxies**. Our galaxy is the 'Milky Way' and it has about 250 000 000 000 stars. The biggest galaxy has about 100 000 000 000 000 stars.

Universe The universe is the whole of space as we know it.

Light speed If you switch on a torch, the beam of light crosses the room at 300 000 (three hundred thousand) kilometres per second. This is so fast that it looks as if it arrives immediately.

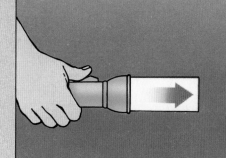

Did you know?
● Nothing can go faster than light. Other beams, like radio waves, also go at this speed. None of our rockets go anywhere near as fast. So the quickest way to contact someone in space is to send a radio signal or a light signal.

The creation of the Earth

This is what the Earth looks like from space. The picture was taken by astronauts on board the Apollo 17 rocket on their way to the Moon.

From space the sky looks black even in the daytime. To us on the ground it looks blue. This is because we are looking up into the Earth's **atmosphere**. The atmosphere is a layer of dust and gas around the planet. The gas sparkles in the light from the Sun and this makes it look blue.

'From the Moon, our planet looks like a little blue marble. If I held out my hand, I could cover the Earth with my thumb.'

Astronaut James Irwin

1 More than 4600 million years ago, wisps of dust and gas spun around our newly formed Sun. The swirling dust gathered into balls. Gradually nine planets began to take shape.

2 The outer planets were huge and gassy. The planets nearer the Sun were small and rocky. The new-born Earth was one of these inner planets. All the time more rocks were smashing into it, pulled down by its force of gravity. The rocks squeezed against each other and became hot.

3 Some of the rocks were so hot that they melted. Slowly the heavier material sank through the bubbling liquid. The lighter rocks floated to the surface where they made a thin crust. There were continuous earthquakes and raging volcanoes. Fiery lava burst through cracks in the crust.

4 Dust and steam and gas hissed out of the ground. The gas drifted upwards and this gas became the Earth's atmosphere. Slowly the blackness of space was hidden by a blue sky.

5 The Earth was now cooling down. Steam in the atmosphere turned into water. It began to rain. The rain lasted millions of years. Slowly the puddles merged into lakes. Then the lakes became seas and finally the seas became oceans.

6 Life began in the oceans. The Earth was now 20 million years old. The first life was a tiny, single cell. Then plants began to develop. After plants came fish. At last, 4400 million years after the Earth's creation, the first mammals were born.

Suppose you could travel back in time 4000 years. Here's what an ancient Egyptian would say about the universe.

The stars 'At night, a beautiful goddess arches over us. Her robe is decorated with sparkling sequins and these are the stars.'

The Sun 'Every day a horse-drawn chariot drives across the sky. In the back of the chariot is a fire and this is the Sun.'

The Earth 'The Earth is a flat round plate.'

This is not what a modern astronomer would say. What has made people change their minds?

The shape of the Earth

Discovery 1 2000 years ago, the Greeks noticed that when they looked straight up, they saw different stars from different places.

Discovery 2 Hundreds of years ago, coastguards noticed that they could always see the top of a ship's mast before the rest of the ship. These are clues that the Earth is round.

Challenge Can you see why?

Discovery 3 In 1520, Ferdinand Magellan sailed right around the Earth. Obviously the Earth was not flat!

Challenge Which shape could be the answer: a cube, a ball, a tube?

Nowadays satellites have circled the Earth and photographed it from every angle. The Earth is round like a ball.

The Egyptian goddess Nut leaning over the Earth

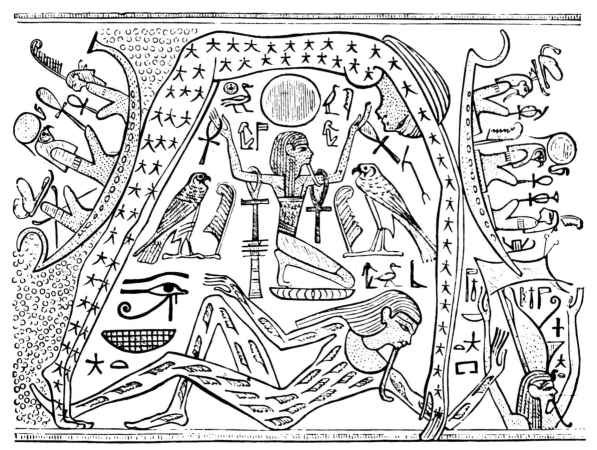

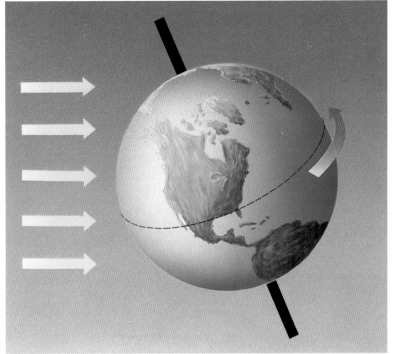

Day and night

The Sun shines in the daytime. At night the sky is dark. What has happened to the Sun? *Challenge* How could you show that the Sun actually shines all the time?

We now know that the Earth spins and this makes night and day. As the Earth turns, the Sun seems to rise in the East, move across the sky and then set in the West.

Diagram to explain day and night

Telling the time

The first sundial was probably just a stick in the ground. Looking at the length and position of the shadow gave a rough idea of the time. Later, sundials became much more sophisticated. *Challenge* Why does the shadow change? When do you get the shortest shadow?

A stick sundial

Time zones

If you want to telephone friends in another country, you should check first what time it is for them. There are 24 'time zones' around the world. In each zone, all the clocks should say the same time. In the zone next door, the time is different by one hour. This system began in 1884 and it is called **Greenwich Mean Time**. The clock which decided what all the other clocks around the world should say was in Greenwich, London.

The seasons

The Greeks thought the Earth was at the very centre of the universe. They said everything else, including the Sun and stars, went around us.

About 500 years ago, a Polish astronomer, **Copernicus**, said that the Earth was turning. He then suggested that all the planets went around the Sun. His opinions made him very unpopular because no one wanted to think the Sun was more important than the Earth.

What Copernicus could not explain is WHY all the planets go around the Sun. What stops them from drifting away into space? The man who came up with the answer was **Isaac Newton**.

Shaken to the core!
The story goes that Newton was sitting under an apple tree in his orchard. He was thinking about the planets, when suddenly an apple hit him on the head. 'Gravity!' he said.

Isaac Newton

Gravity

The Earth is a huge ball and yet people on the other side of the Earth don't fall off. They are held on by **gravity**. Gravity is a pulling force and it pulls everything towards the centre of the Earth.

Everything has its own force of gravity. Big things (like the Earth) have a big pulling force, while small things (like chairs and tables) have a tiny force.

The Sun's force of gravity is so strong that it reaches across space to the planets.

The planets cannot drift away, because the Sun's force of gravity pulls them back.

Gravity is also the force which holds the Moon in orbit around the Earth.

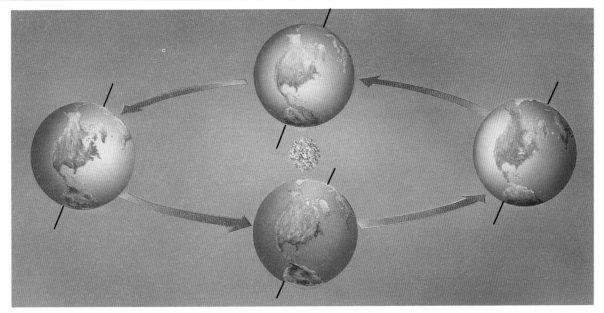

Earth's orbit around the Sun

The seasons

The Earth takes one year to go once around the Sun. At the same time, the Earth turns on its axis. It takes one day to turn once. The Earth's axis is tipped.

In summer The North Pole points towards the Sun. Britain is in sunlight for a long time each day.

In winter The Earth has moved to the other side of the Sun. Now the North Pole points outwards. Britain spends most of the day in darkness.

Challenge That's how it works for the Northern Hemisphere. What about Australia in the Southern Hemisphere?

Have you noticed that summer sunshine feels warmer than winter sunshine?

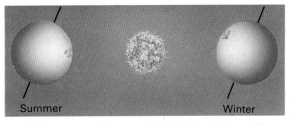

Summer   Winter

In summer The sunshine is falling flat on the land.

In winter Sunshine is falling at an angle. You can feel the effect on your hands near a bonfire. With your palms tipped, you feel less heat than if your palms are flat to the flames.

Astronomical dictionary

Axis The Earth turns on its axis. Imagine threading a bead onto a needle and then spinning the bead. The needle is the bead's axis.

The Poles At the top of the Earth's axis is the North Pole and at the bottom is the South Pole.

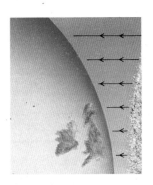

Summer sunshine

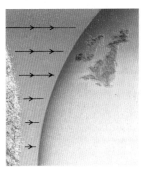

Winter sunshine

The sundial

The easiest way to make a sundial is to stand a stick in the ground and then mark its shadow with a stone every hour. Label each stone with the time. From the next day onwards you can find out the time by looking at the position of the shadow. (Of course it's no good if the Sun isn't shining!) If you want a more interesting sundial you could make this 'bottle sundial'.

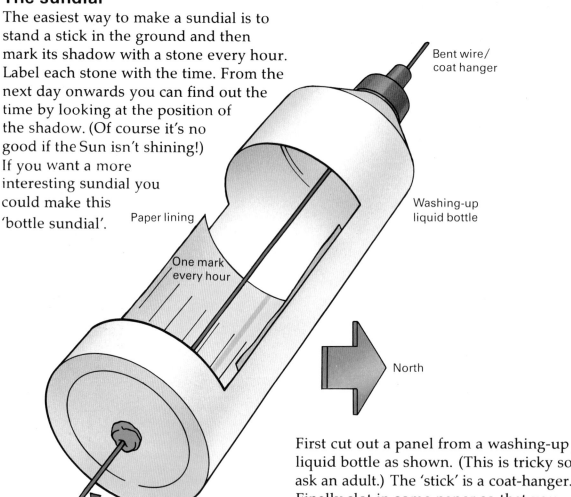

Bent wire/coat hanger

Washing-up liquid bottle

Paper lining

One mark every hour

North

52°

Support bricks

North

52°

Latitude of Britain

Sun

52°

Equator

First cut out a panel from a washing-up liquid bottle as shown. (This is tricky so ask an adult.) The 'stick' is a coat-hanger. Finally slot in some paper so that you can mark the shadow every hour as before. If you make both sundials you should find this one has an advantage over the plain stick. What is it?

To catch as much sunlight as possible, the bottle should face into the Sun. The Earth is curved and Britain is quite far up the curve. If you leave the bottle flat on the ground, it will actually be tipping away from the Sun. Your **latitude** tells you how much the ground is tipped where you are. For example, Britain is at a latitude of 52 degrees, the North Pole is at 90 and the Equator is at zero degrees.

Finally, the end of the bottle should point North.

Comparing summer and winter sunshine

You need a torch and a football. Firstly point the torch at the middle of the ball. This is like sunlight in summer.

Now move the torch upwards but don't tip the torch. The patch of light spreads out and looks fainter. This is like winter sunshine.

Can you see why countries around the Equator are hotter than countries near the North and South Poles?

If you draw circles on the ball like the circles of latitude, you can investigate the effect of the Earth's tipped axis. Stick blobs on the ball to represent Britain and Australia. Then tip the ball and turn it. Which way do you need to tip the ball to get winter in Australia?

Gravity

For this investigation you need a short piece of string and something like a conker tied to the end.

To keep something moving in a circle requires force. Without that force, the object would fly off. Similarly, the Earth is able to circle the Sun because of the pulling force of gravity.

In the case of a whirling conker, your hand supplies the force by pulling on the string. What would happen if you let go?

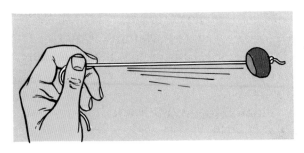

Did you know?
- It actually takes the Earth 365¼ days to go around the Sun. So every four years, an extra day is put into the year. That day is 29 February. The year is called a **Leap Year**. 1992 is a leap year.

- In the Northern Hemisphere, the 'longest day' is 21 June. On this day, the North Pole is pointing directly at the Sun and we have the longest time of daylight. The longest time of darkness comes six months later – on 22 December.

- The Earth still has a liquid layer underneath its solid crust. Huge bits of the crust move around and sometimes rub against each other. This causes **earthquakes**.

The Sun

Without the Sun there would be no life on Earth. The Sun provides light and heat. Its powerful force of gravity keeps the planets in their orbits.

The Sun's core

The Sun is the hottest object in the solar system. It is mainly made of a gas called hydrogen. Deep inside the Sun, the hydrogen is turned into another gas, helium. The change is called **Nuclear Fusion** and it makes an enormous amount of heat. Scientists are trying to make nuclear fusion work in laboratories on Earth. The Sun is so hot that it shines like a white hot flame. The temperature in the Sun's core is thought to be over 15 million °C.

The Sun's lifetime

The Sun will last another 5000 million years. (At the moment it is halfway through its life.) As its hydrogen runs out, it will puff up until it becomes a hundred times bigger. The inner planets, including the Earth, will be swallowed up. Then the surface layer of the Sun will be blown off into space. Meanwhile the rest will shrink back into a hot white ball. Slowly the Sun will cool down. Eventually, nothing will remain but a cold brown husk. (By this time, humans will probably have moved to another solar system!)

> **Did you know?**
> - The Sun's diameter is about 100 times bigger than the Earth's.
>
> - The disturbances caused by flares can reach across space to the Earth. They are picked up as radio crackle.

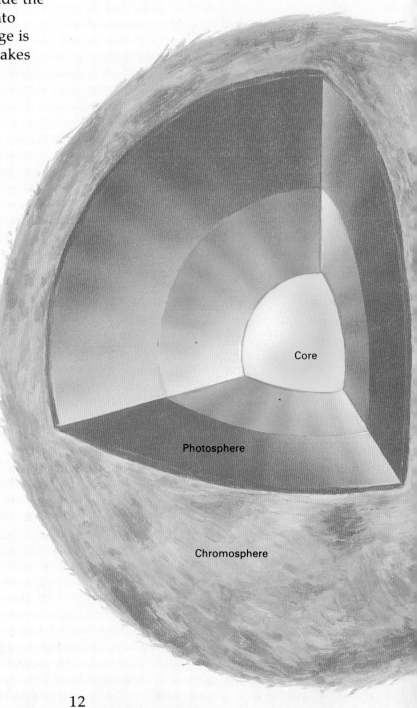

Core

Photosphere

Chromosphere

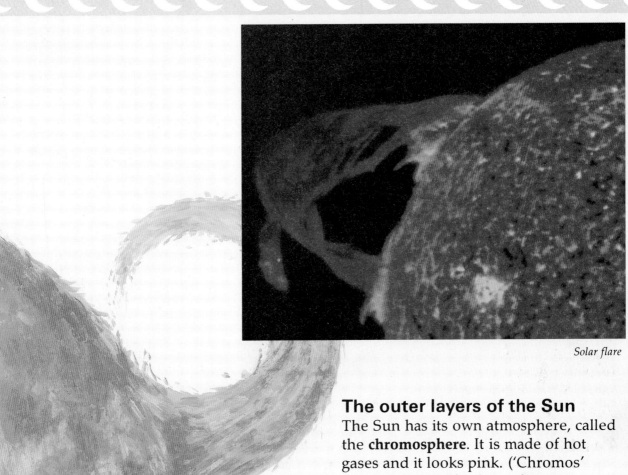

Solar flare

Flare

Sunspots

Prominences

The outer layers of the Sun

The Sun has its own atmosphere, called the **chromosphere**. It is made of hot gases and it looks pink. ('Chromos' means coloured.) Above the chromosphere, there is a second, thinner atmosphere, called the **corona**.

The photosphere

The surface layer of the Sun is made of boiling gas. It is this layer that gives out light. It is called the **photosphere**. ('Photos' means light.)

Sunspots

Sometimes dark patches appear on the surface; these are **sunspots**. They are the sites of violent storms. The flares are called **prominences**.

Light

The Sun is the only thing in the solar system which gives out light of its own. The Moon only seems to shine because it glints in the Sun's light.

13

The surface of the Moon

The Moon was made at about the same time as the Earth – 4600 million years later, the Earth is bustling with life. The Moon is grey, lifeless and frozen. Why have the two planets changed into such vastly different worlds?

No atmosphere

The Moon is much smaller than the Earth. Like most small planets, it doesn't have an atmosphere. Its sky is black. No atmosphere also means that the Moon is silent, because sound waves cannot travel through empty space. The lunar astronauts could only talk to each other through their radios.

Frozen and baked

The Moon turns on its axis once every 27 days. So the land is in daylight for about two weeks and then in darkness for the next two weeks. Without an atmosphere to protect it, the ground gets hotter and hotter. It reaches 110 degrees Celsius, which is hotter than boiling water. Then in the long lunar night, the temperature drops to minus 150 degrees Celsius, which is far, far below freezing.

The far side   The Moon turns so that the same side of its surface always faces the Earth. It wasn't until October 1959 that the far side was photographed by **Lunik 3**, a Russian space craft.

No water

When astronomers first gazed at the Moon, they thought they could see oceans and lakes. In fact these 'lakes' were dry, dusty craters. If there ever was water on the Moon, it must have evaporated long ago.

Without water and without air, there can be no life.

Moon landing

The first human footprint on the Moon was made by an American, **Neil Armstrong**, in 1969. Altogether, twelve people have walked across the Moon. Their footprints and the clutter of flags have remained there unchanged ever since.

Damage by meteorites

The moon is covered in grey, dusty craters. The craters are made by **meteorites**. These are bits of rubble that are floating around in space. If they pass too close to the Moon, they are pulled down by its force of gravity. Meteorites also plunge towards the Earth, but they usually burn up in the Earth's atmosphere. We see them occasionally as shooting stars.

An astronaut at work on the Moon

Did you know?

● There is no air on the Moon to blow the dust around. So the craters and the astronauts' footprints are never filled in.

● On the Moon, you could jump six times higher than on Earth, because of the low gravity.

● Many of the craters on the near side of the Moon have watery names, like the Sea of Cold, the Ocean of Storms and the Lake of Dreams.

● The distance to the Moon is about 384 000 kilometres. This is about the same as going ten times round the Earth.

Earth, Sun and Moon

Just as the Earth goes around the Sun, so the Moon goes around the Earth. It turns very slowly as it goes, so that the same side is always facing the Earth. This is why we always see the familiar 'face' of the Moon.

Sizes   The Earth is four times wider than the Moon. The Sun is 100 times wider than the Earth and 400 times wider than the Moon. It is also 400 times further away and this means that it looks about the same size as the moon in the sky.

The phases of the Moon

Sometimes we see a full round Moon and sometimes just a crescent. Read on to find out why.

The Moon does not give out any light of its own, it is lit by sunlight. The side of the Moon facing the Sun is lit while the other side is in darkness.

From the Earth, sometimes we can see all of this lit side – **a full Moon**. Sometimes we can only see a bit of it – **a crescent Moon**. As the Moon travels around the Earth, the amount we see changes.

Phases of the Moon

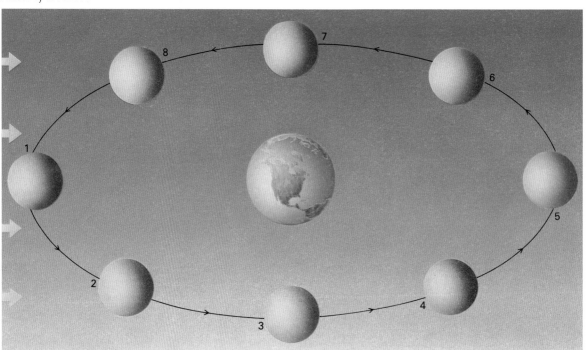

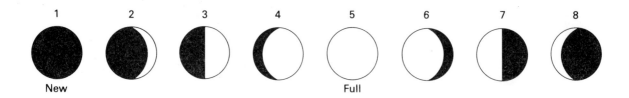

16

An eclipse

If the Moon lines up with the Sun, it can completely cover it up. For a short time, an area of the Earth becomes as dark as night. This is a **solar eclipse**. Astronomers take advantage of such occasions to study the Sun's atmosphere. Normally the atmosphere is hidden by the dazzling light from the Sun's surface. During an eclipse, the Sun is covered and only the prominences and atmosphere around the edge can be seen.

More common than total eclipses are partial eclipses. This is when the Moon just covers a bit of the Sun as it passes.

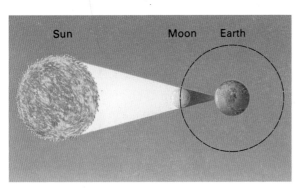

Eclipse of the Sun

Lunar eclipse   During a **lunar eclipse**, the Moon goes behind the Earth so that it is hidden from the Sun's light. Solar and lunar eclipses happen on average three or four times a year.

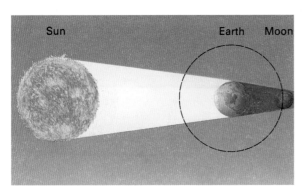

Eclipse of the Moon

The tides

The Earth's pull of gravity keeps the Moon from flying away. At the same time, the Moon's gravity tugs on the Earth. It pulls the oceans towards it and this makes the tides. See the diagram below:

How the Moon affects the Earth's tides

Did you know?
- The Moon orbits the Earth in 27 days.

- The Moon travels at 3660 kilometres an hour around the Earth.

- The Moon, Earth and Sun are back in the same positions, relative to each other, every 18 years, 11 days.

- 98 per cent of the matter in the solar system is crammed into the Sun. The Earth and Moon together take less than one hundredth of what's left.

Lunar experiments

An eclipse

Don't confuse an eclipse of the Moon with the phases of the Moon. In an eclipse, the Moon ducks into the Earth's shadow. The round shape of the Earth's shadow across the Moon was one of the things that persuaded ancient astronomers that the Earth was round.

Eclipses are rare. Usually the Moon goes slightly above or below the Earth's shadow. Meanwhile the phases of the Moon happen every month.

Investigation You can investigate the phases with a ball or orange. Stand, facing a shaft of light, and hold the ball out. Then turn on the spot. The ball is the Moon and your head is the Earth. You should see a new Moon, then a crescent, then a full Moon and finally a crescent. To see the full Moon, you need to lift the ball clear of your shadow. If you move the ball into your shadow, you are seeing an eclipse.

Meteoric spuds!

Potato prints make excellent craters. For the best results, cut out a circle of dark grey paper and put white paint on the potato. You could use the picture below for reference and make a map of the Moon's near side.

Lunar landscapes

To get a close look at the shape of a meteorite crater, put a layer of icing sugar or flour into a tall baking tray. Then drop 'meteorites' into the tray. The Moon's craters come in all sizes – from a couple of centimetres to over 230 kilometres wide. So try dropping marbles, a tomato, an orange, beads . . . .

Lunar dictionary

Waxing and waning   The Moon **waxes** as we see it get larger and brighter. It **wanes** as it grows smaller.

Meteorite   Meteorites come in all shapes and sizes. Many are as small as a grain of sand. They are bits of debris, left over when the planets were formed. While in space, they are called **meteoroids** and if they strike a planet, they are called **meteorites**.

Did you know?

- A few meteorites survive the fall through the Earth's atmosphere. In the Arizona desert there is a crater 1250 metres wide by 175 metres deep. It was made by a massive meteorite which pounded into the Earth 25 000 years ago.

- There are two kinds of meteorite – stony meteorites made of rock and metallic meteorites made of iron and nickel. A metallic meteorite was found in Africa which weighs over 60 tonnes.

- The Earth is not the only planet to have a Moon. Pluto has 1, Jupiter has at least 15 and Saturn has over 21.

The Arizona meteor crater. See the car park for scale!

Living in space

Weightlessness in space

To live in space, astronauts need a supply of air, food and drinking water. They must also be prepared for 'weightlessness'.

Weightlessness

It's hard to imagine life without gravity. Astronauts can float about freely. Before they go to sleep, they must strap themselves to their beds so that they don't drift around the capsule. To move about, they just push off the wall and they can then float from one end of the capsule to the other.

Space-sickness

Weightlessness is exciting but it can also be extremely uncomfortable. Many astronauts get puffy faces because their blood is not being pulled towards their feet. (You'll know how that feels if you've ever hung upside down!) Without weight, their bodies stretch. They become about 5 centimetres taller. Their arm and leg muscles become weak as they are not moving them against gravity. Their bones get thin and delicate.

Training before the mission helps the astronauts to cope. Once back on Earth, their bodies soon recover.

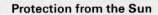

Designing for space

Things that are easy to do on Earth become terribly difficult in space. Suppose you want a glass of orange juice. You can't tip the drink out of the glass into your mouth. Even if you turn the glass upside down, the drink will stay inside.

For the Apollo missions, drinks were put into bags with spouts. The astronauts could squeeze the drink into their mouths.

Meals must be carefully planned. Crumbly food is dangerous because the crumbs float away. Some food comes in powder form so that it takes up less space. The astronauts add water before the meal. All the menus have to be planned in advance to make sure they give a balanced diet.

An ordinary lavatory would not work in space. During the early space missions, astronauts had to use sticky tape to catch body wastes. Later, the space-shuttle was fitted with a specially designed toilet with air jets.

Space food

Protection from the Sun
The suit is white to reflect the Sun's fierce rays. It is made of tough plastic. Inside the plastic is a thin metal layer. This is to stop the astronaut from being hurt by a meteorite storm.

The visor
The visor is tinted to cut down sunlight.

Gloves
The gloves screw tightly onto the suit's sleeves. This makes sure that air cannot escape through the join.

Joints
The suit must be flexible so that the astronaut can bend and walk.

Liquid-cooled underwear
To stop the astronaut from overheating, a pair of long-johns is fitted with plastic tubes full of cold water.

Rubber inner layer

The back pack
In the backpack is water, air and a radio for communicating.

The space suit

Sometimes the astronauts leave the space capsule – for example, to explore the Moon, or to mend the capsule. Their space suits must supply everything they need to survive.

The rocket

To get into space you need a rocket. A rocket can overcome the Earth's gravity. It can lift itself, its cargo, its passengers and its fuel off the ground – and then continue to climb into space.

The rocket engine has three parts, or stages.

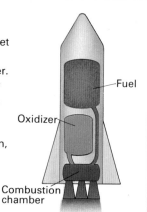

The first rocket
The first workable rocket was designed by a Russian schoolteacher. Konstantin Tsiolkovsky drew a rocket in 1903, but he never actually built one. Twenty-five years later, an American, Robert Goddard, went on the first rocket test flight.

Fuel

Oxidizer

Combustion chamber

The three-stage rocket
It needs an enormous amount of gas to get off the Earth. The rocket burns several tonnes of fuel every second. In fact, before take-off, most of the rocket is fuel!

Earth transport

Out of a car, an aeroplane, a boat and a rocket, the rocket is the only machine that works in space. The others move by pushing against something around them. The car's wheels push the road. The boat's propeller pushes the water and the aeroplane's wings push the air. In space there is no air, land or water. The rocket carries everything it needs on board. It lifts itself by throwing gas through its thrusters.

How the rocket works

If you stood on a skateboard and threw a pillow forward, the skateboard would jerk backwards. Newton realised that if you push something one way, you yourself are pushed in the opposite direction. Pushing gas downwards pushes the rocket up.

Apollo mission to the Moon

In 1969, for the very first time, humans landed on the Moon. It was an American space mission, in a rocket called **Apollo 11**.

Once the Apollo was in orbit round the Moon, two of the astronauts moved into the tiny lunar lander. They separated the 'Eagle' from the main rocket and set off for the Moon. *'The Eagle has landed,'* said Buzz Aldrin. *'We're breathing again – thanks a lot,'* said Mission Control.

The Command Module separates from the third stage. Once all the fuel in a stage is used up, that stage is thrown away.

By the time the rocket returns to Earth, only a small nose capsule is left.

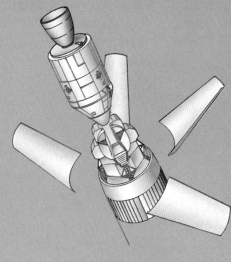

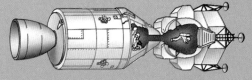

Buzz Aldrin walking on the Moon

A few moments later, Neil Armstrong was the first person to tread on lunar soil. Altogether the astronauts spent two and a half hours on the Moon. First they collected rock samples. Then they set up an American flag and filmed each other leaping about. The easiest way to move in the low gravity was by kangaroo hopping. Finally they put down a box of messages sent from leaders on Earth. These will stay on the Moon in case any other life forms pass by our way.

Once Neil and Buzz were safely back in the main rocket, the lunar lander was ejected. By the time the astronauts reached Earth, all that was left of the great Apollo rocket was its tiny nose compartment. Parachutes carried the 'Command Module' gently down sea where a recovery ship was w The first lunar mission was safe

Exploring space

At this very moment, there are hundreds of space stations and satellites up in space. Many will stay up for years. Do you know what they are used for, how they got there and why they don't fall down?

Defying gravity

There is a well-known phrase – 'What goes up must come down'. Yet some satellites may never come down.

These satellites race around the Earth at an amazing 28 000 kilometres an hour – that's 11 times faster than Concorde. Gravity **is** pulling them down, but they are going forward so fast that they overshoot the Earth's surface. They circle round and round. They are in **Orbit**. Satellites must go so fast to stay in orbit that some are racing around the Earth in an hour and a half.

The first man-made satellite was launched by the Russians in 1957. **Sputnik 1** was a metal ball, just 58 centimetres wide.

The Earth's biggest satellite is the Moon. It has stayed in orbit for the longest – about 4600 million years.

Into orbit

Satellites are taken into space and launched by a rocket. It's important that they stay above the Earth's atmosphere, where there is no air to slow them down. In this case they can keep going for months without needing to boost their speeds. If they do slow down, they quickly spiral to Earth.

Spies in the skies
Satellites are launched a few hundred kilometres above the Earth. Some are weather satellites, looking at things like cloud patterns. Communications satellites bounce television and telephone signals around the Earth. Other satellites are pointing upwards. The Hubble Space Telescope is looking at distant stars and galaxies.

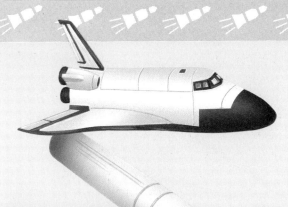

The space shuttle
Building a new rocket for every mission was getting expensive. So the Americans designed a reusable rocket.

The 'space shuttle' carries a large tank of fuel which is dropped about eight minutes after take-off. This is the only part which is thrown away each time.

The rest of the rocket continues into orbit where it launches its cargo. Finally the Shuttle glides back to Earth, to be prepared for another trip.

Space laboratories

Things in orbit are 'weightless'. They are free to float around the space capsule, as if there was no gravity. Which way will a plant grow without gravity pulling it down? How will a spider spin its web? Do crystals grow differently? There are many experiments scientists wanted to try in this strange environment and so scientific laboratories were taken into orbit.

The first space laboratory was the American **Skylab**. It was launched in 1973. Skylab was built from the leftovers of the Apollo projects.

In 1983 **Spacelab** was launched. It is a joint European and American project. The laboratory can be carried in the **space shuttle**. The idea is that it can be taken into space many times with different sets of experiments.

Astronaut working outside the space craft

The satellite

Satellites come in all shapes and sizes. They are above the Earth's atmosphere (where there is no air). This means they can have delicate instruments sticking out on poles. (Imagine strapping such a satellite to the roof of a car and driving it fast down the motorway. The air rushing past would soon snap the instruments off.)

To make a model satellite, you could copy Landsat 4 on the previous page, or you could design your own satellite. A milk bottle top makes a good radio antenna and cardboard strips covered in baking foil look like the solar panels.

Decide whether the satellite is a communications, weather or astronomy satellite and try to think of instruments for it.

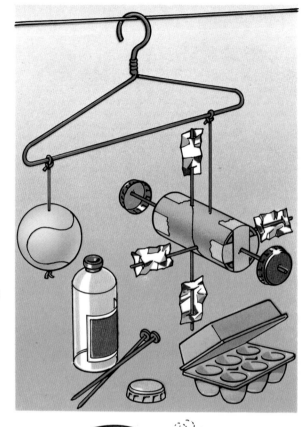

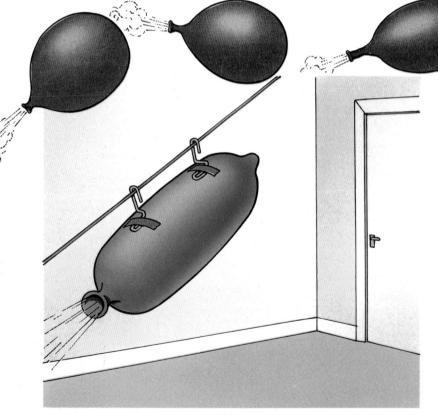

The rocket

The rocket moves by pushing gas through its nozzles. You can get a balloon to do the same kind of thing. If you blow up the balloon and let go, the air rushes out and the balloon zigzags around the room. Now fix up a wire or cotton line so that it slopes upwards and across the room. If you hook the balloon onto the line, it can only go in one direction. This 'rocket' can overcome gravity and shoot upwards.

The conquest of space

- The first object to go into orbit was the Russian metal ball, Sputnik 1, in 1957.

- A month later, the first living thing went into space. Laika the dog orbited the Earth in the Russian rocket Sputnik 2.

- The first human in space was a Russian cosmonaut, **Yuri Gagarin**. He went into orbit in 1961. Two years later, **Valentina Tereshkova** (also Russian) became the first woman in space.

- In 1965 the first 'space walk' was made by yet another Russian, Alexei Leonov. He spent 20 minutes outside his spacecraft Voshkod 2.

- The Russians were in competition with the Americans to do everything first in space. Just when the Russians thought they were definitely winning, two American astronauts became the first people to land on the Moon. That was in 1969. Now the question is: who will be first to land on Mars?

A rocket takes off from the Kennedy Space Center

Mercury and Venus

Diagram to show relative sizes of the planets.

Suppose you could choose which planet in our solar system you wanted to live on. There are nine to consider. Some are frozen, while some are hotter than melting lead. Some are entirely covered in liquid. Pluto is smaller than our Moon, while Jupiter is twice as massive as all the other planets put together. You mustn't choose the Earth, so which one will you go for?

Facts about Mercury
- Daytime temperature: 350°C
- Night-time temperature: −170°C
- Number of moons: none
- Ever visited?
An American space probe, Mariner 10, flew past Mercury in 1974 and took photographs. These were sent to Earth by radio signals.

Mercury

Mercury is the second smallest planet and lies closest to the Sun. In the daytime, the surface is as hot as an oven. The bare rocks are dazzlingly bright in the fierce sunlight. Mercury turns very slowly. During its long night, the temperature plunges far below freezing.

If you stood on Mercury you would see the bumps and pits of meteorite craters. There are also deep cracks which appeared when the planet first formed.

Venus

Venus is one of the hottest places in the solar system. It is about the same size as the Earth. Unlike the Earth, it has a very thick cloudy atmosphere. The clouds let sunlight in and the sunlight heats up the ground. The heat, however, cannot get back out through the clouds. It is trapped. So the ground gets hotter and hotter. This is called the 'greenhouse' effect.

Saturn   Uranus   Neptune   Pluto

The clouds are not made of water but of acid. When the Russian space probes, Venera 9 and 10, landed on Venus, they lasted for only an hour before the heavy acidic air silenced them forever.

When the planets first formed, Venus was like the Earth. On Earth, tiny plants living in the oceans made oxygen – the gas which animals breathe. On Venus, which is closer to the Sun, the oceans boiled away. Plant-life never began and the planet was left with its original choking atmosphere. Choose Venus at your peril!

The Earth
The third planet from the Sun is the Earth.

Facts about Earth
- One year: 365 days
- Average temperature: 22°C
- Atmosphere: mainly nitrogen and oxygen

Facts about Venus
- Average temperature: 465°C
- Number of moons: none
- Atmosphere: carbon dioxide
- Composition: iron core, mantle and rocky crust (like Earth).

THESE ARE THE DIAMETERS OF THE PLANETS FOR REFERENCE.

Mercury	5 thousand million km
Venus	12 thousand million km
Earth	12 thousand million km
Mars	7 thousand million km
Jupiter	143 thousand million km
Saturn	120 thousand million km
Uranus	52 thousand million km
Neptune	48 thousand million km
Pluto	4 thousand million km

Mars

Mars is probably the planet humans will visit first. Until recently scientists hoped to find life on Mars. It is colder than Earth, but it **has** got an atmosphere and water. Early astronomers thought they could see canals which might have been dug by intelligent beings.

Since then, space probes have landed on Mars. The water is frozen at the poles. Most scientists think the canals were formed naturally and then dried up millions of years ago. The probes could find no signs of life.

A Martian day is only 37 minutes longer than a day on Earth. The atmosphere is thin which means the ground gets very hot. At night, it suddenly gets very cold.

Like the Earth, Mars has seasons. Its axis is tilted by 24 degrees. In the summer there are violent dust storms, which can spread across the whole planet.

Facts about Mars
- Average temperature: −23°C
- Number of moons: 2
- Axis: tilted to 24 degrees
- Ever visited? The Viking probes landed on Mars in 1976. They photographed the surface and tested the soil for signs of life.

Mars, with its orange sky and red rocky ground.

Jupiter: the 'great red spot' is the site of an enormous swirling hurricane, which itself is the size of the Earth.

Jupiter

Jupiter is twice as massive as all the other planets added together. It's often called the 'gas giant'. Jupiter is mostly made of layers of gas and liquid. The only solid part is a small rocky core in the planet's centre.

Jupiter spins in less than 10 hours. This causes terrific storms in its frothy oceans. The heat does not come from the Sun. It is made inside the planet itself. If Jupiter had been a few times bigger, it might have become a Sun.

Facts about Jupiter
- Temperature: −150°C at the top of the atmosphere; 30 000°C at the core.
- Number of moons: at least 15

The outer planets

Jupiter, Saturn, Uranus, Neptune and Pluto are known as the outer planets

Saturn

Saturn is famous for its rings. It is another gas giant like Jupiter, but slightly smaller. Under layers of hazy cloud is a stormy ocean.

The rings are made of lumps of ice which are in orbit around the planet. Some lumps are as big as houses, while others are tiny flakes. The outermost ring may be a broken-up moon. The others are probably rubble which was left over when the planet first formed.

The bright rings of Saturn

Saturn, like Jupiter, spins very quickly. This causes winds which blow at an amazing 1800 km an hour. Bands of cloud are whirled around the planet. If you pick Saturn, you're in for a stormy ride.

Facts about Saturn
- Number of moons: about 23
- Ever visited? Voyager 1 and 2 were launched in 1977. They travelled right across the solar system, passing Jupiter, Saturn, Uranus and Neptune.

Uranus

Uranus is the third largest planet in the solar system, but it is much smaller than Jupiter and Saturn. The whole planet is smothered in a thick, blue-green fog. Its surface is covered in a swirling ocean.

Uranus is unusual because its axis is very tilted. Astronomers think it may have been hit by an asteroid. A year on Uranus is 84 Earth years.

Uranus

Right: Diagram to show the comparison in size between Neptune, Pluto and planet Earth.

Left: Neptune

Neptune

Neptune is like Uranus but has a bluer colour. Its surface is covered in a deep ocean. At the moment Neptune is further from the Sun than Pluto. This is because Pluto has a peculiar orbit.

Pluto

The smallest planet in the solar system is about half the size of our Moon. Icy Pluto has its own tiny moon, Charon.

A year on Pluto is 247 Earth years long, because it is so far from the Sun. If you decide to choose Pluto, one thing is certain – it's going to be cold!

Pluto and its tiny moon, Charon

The spacecraft Voyager 2 orbited and photographed many of the planets.

So far humans have not visited any of the planets. Even so, a lot is known about them from pictures sent back by space probes. There are other details scientists can work out.

Gassy giants and rocky midgets   The planets were probably made at the same time as the Sun. They were formed from clouds of drifting space dust.

The asteroids   Any left-over bits of rubble continued to float about in space. These are the asteroids. There is a large collection of asteroids between Mars and Jupiter called the **Asteroid Belt**. These asteroids may be bits of a broken-up planet.

A year   All the planets circle the Sun anti-clockwise. The outer planets move more slowly than the inner ones and they also have further to go. A year on Neptune is 600 times longer than a year on Mercury. It is 80 times further away.

Temperature   The most important factor is the planet's distance from the Sun. On Mercury the temperature reaches 400°C in the daytime. On Neptune it is −220°C.

Atmosphere   An atmosphere soaks up some of the Sun's rays and stops a planet from getting too hot. At night it works like a blanket, trapping in some of the heat. Smaller planets usually don't have atmospheres. At night they lose their heat into space and quickly become very cold.

Mercury and Mars have thin atmospheres. Enormous Jupiter has a thick atmosphere, while tiny Pluto has no atmosphere at all.

PLANET	LENGTH OF ORBIT (Earth days)	TEMPERATURE
Mercury	88 Earth days	from −170 to 350°C
Venus	225 Earth days	465°C
Earth	365 days	22°C
Mars	almost 2 Earth years	−23°C
Jupiter	12 Earth years	−150°C
Saturn	30 Earth years	−180°C
Uranus	84 Earth years	−210°C
Neptune	165 Earth years	−220°C
Pluto	248 Earth years	−220°C

Did you know?

- A day on Venus is longer than a year on Venus. (Venus takes longer to spin than to orbit the Sun.)
- A tin can would melt on the surface of Mercury.
- Jupiter is so big, it could swallow 1300 Earths!
- Neptune was named after the Roman god of the sea, because it looked so blue. Only later did astronomers discover it really is a watery planet.

Planet quiz

1 Which planet is the smallest?
2 Which planet is closest to the Sun?
3 Venus is stiflingly hot because of the .... effect.
4 Jupiter is known as the ....
5 The Earth is the .... planet from the Sun.
6 How many planets are there?

Cardboard Solar System

The planets are spread far across the solar system. This investigation will show you just how much space is between each. Choose a long clear wall, for example in your bedroom and measure out these distances:

Sun	0 cm	Mercury	3 cm
Venus	6 cm	Earth	8½ cm
Mars	12 cm	Jupiter	43 cm
Saturn	79 cm	Uranus	140 cm
Neptune	250 cm	Pluto	330 cm

Mark each position with a tiny blob of blue tack.

Now how big do you think the planets are on this scale? In fact, the biggest planet, Jupiter, is smaller than this full stop. Even your little blobs are too big!

If you want to see the planets at all, you have to cheat and make them bigger than they should be.
Trace the planets from page 28 onto a sheet of paper and colour them. Stick the sheet to a cereal packet and cut out the circles. Now stick these to the points you've already marked.
By the way, on this scale, the Sun is nearly as big as you are!

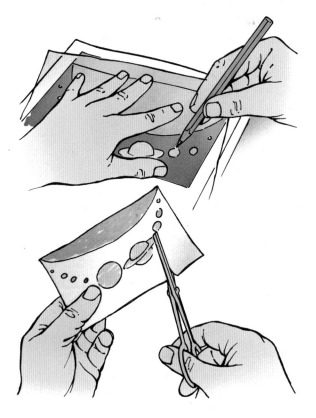

Earthlings have stared into space for thousands of years. In all that time the stars have barely changed, but peoples' ideas have changed completely.

Ancient astronomers 4000 years ago, the Egyptians thought the stars were sequins. Nowadays astronomers think they are gigantic fireballs of gas, scattered enormous distances across the universe.

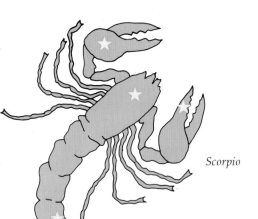

Scorpio

Pisces

Leo

Gemini

Constellations

On a clear night, you can see about 2000 stars without a telescope. The Romans grouped certain stars together to make shapes. These shapes are the 'constellations'. They have Latin names like 'Ursa Major' which means 'Great Bear'. There is also 'Pisces' (the fish), 'Leo' (the lion) and 'Taurus' (the bull). All the constellations together are known as 'the Zodiac', which means 'the Animals'!

Star signs   Your 'star-sign' is the name of the constellation which was above you on the day you were born. Every year, on that date, the Earth gets to the same place in its orbit. These stars are overhead again. They mark your birthday as surely as the date. Unfortunately they are also the very stars you can't see at the time. They are overhead literally on the DAY of your birth (not the night) so they are blocked out by the Sun. If you want to see them, you must wait six months!

Fortune telling   During the year the constellations move around the sky. Ancient stargazers thought this was a coded message to tell them about the future.

Time-lapse photograph to show the movement of the stars

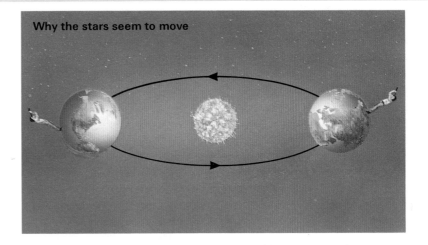

Why the stars seem to move

Why the stars seem to move

The pattern of stars moves for two reasons. Firstly, it changes during the night. The Earth is spinning at night as well as in the day. So just as the Sun seems to move during the day, the stars move round us during the night.

Secondly the pattern changes during the year. All the time, the Earth is moving along its orbit round the Sun. Every night we are looking outwards on a slightly different set of stars. Compared to the summer, by winter we are looking out in the opposite direction.

Aries

Gas Nebulae

It turns out that our Sun is a very ordinary star in the universe. Astronomers have now seen stars which are bigger, smaller, brighter and dimmer. They have also found spinning stars, exploding stars and even possibly Black Holes.

Star birth   Stars are made inside enormous clouds of gas and dust. Bits of gas start drifting into each other. They squash together to make a giant ball. Eventually the ball is squeezed so tightly that changes begin to happen deep inside. There is a sudden blaze of light. The ball of gas is now a star.

White dwarfs   The star changes the hydrogen gas inside it into other things. A small star uses its gas slowly and lives a long time. After about 10 000 million years it puffs up into a red giant.

The giant can be a hundred times bigger than the old star. The outer layers are blown off, while the rest of the star shrinks back to become a small white dwarf. The dwarf star cools and fades.

Supernovas   Giant stars are like furious bonfires. While they last, they are extremely hot, but they soon race through their hydrogen supply. Suddenly there is an enormous flash and the star explodes. The explosion is called a 'supernova'.

Pulsars   Sometimes a giant star is not completely destroyed in the explosion. The middle is left behind and may become a spinning star. As it spins, it gives out a powerful beam of light which sweeps round the sky. From Earth it looks like the flashing beacon of a lighthouse. The star is called a Pulsar.

Recycling

Stars turn hydrogen gas into helium gas. They then turn the helium into harder, rockier materials. When the stars blow up, everything goes back into the gas cloud. The next set of stars may have some of this material in them. Our Sun is a grandchild of the very first stars. It has some material that has been recycled twice already.

This is very important for us because the Earth is made of rocky material. In other words, our planet is made of recycled stars.

Did you know?
- In our galaxy a supernova happens once every few hundred years. The explosion is sometimes so bright that it shows up in the daytime.

- It is impossible to see Black Holes. All the same, some astronomers think they have seen signs of them.

- There might be a Black Hole in the centre of our galaxy. (Even if there is, it won't reach us!)

- Most things on Earth are made of 'recycled stars' – including us! Did you know you are made of 'recycled stars'?

Left: Artist's impression of a Black Hole

Black Hole

It is thought that the biggest stars of all might become Black Holes. When a huge star gets near the end of its life, it starts to squash inwards. As it squashes, its force of gravity gets stronger and stronger. Any nearby dust or gas is sucked in by its tremendous pull.

The star goes on squeezing itself ever smaller. Eventually anything that comes too close is dragged in – even light itself. Stars which give out light look white. A star which sucks in light looks black. It is a Black Hole.

Looking at the stars

Ancient astronomers only had their eyes to go by. So perhaps it's not surprising that they didn't know much about the universe. We have got telescopes and invisible-ray detectors to help us find out about space.

The earliest telescope   The first person to use a telescope for looking at the stars was an Italian professor, **Galilei Galileo**, in 1609.

Bright and faint

You may have noticed that some stars look brighter than others. Sometimes this is because the other stars are further away. Remember how car headlights get brighter as they get closer. A second reason is that some stars are bigger and hotter than others. Bigger stars are brighter than smaller stars.

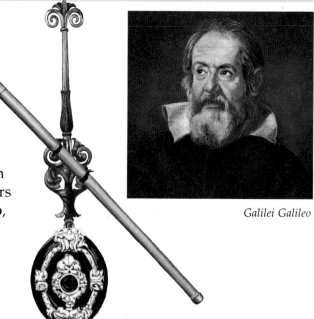

Galilei Galileo

Galileo's telescope. Galileo made many discoveries including the fact that Jupiter had moons

Eye pupil in the light

Eye pupil in the dark

How it works

A telescope makes stars look brighter. In the dark, your eye pupils grow bigger to let in more light. Even so, most stars still look faint. The front of a telescope is much bigger than an eye pupil, so it lets in far more light. Glass lenses then focus the light into your eye. The bigger the telescope, the more light it lets in, which is why many telescopes are so big.

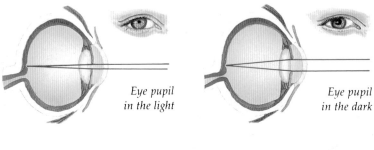

How a big telescope works

Colour coding

Astronomers can tell how hot a star is by its colour. The big hot stars give out slightly blue light. Our Sun is a medium-hot star and it looks bright yellow. Warm stars give out orangey-yellow light. Stars cool down as they get older, so this also helps astronomers work out a star's age.

Invisible rays   Stars give out light, which we can see. They also give out other rays which are invisible to human eyes, for example X-rays, ultra-violet waves, infra-red waves and radio waves.

Infra-red   Many objects that are not hot enough to give out ordinary light, give out invisible infra-red rays. A warm cup of tea gives out infra-red.

There are also objects in space giving out infra-red, for example very old and dying stars. The rays can be picked up by special telescopes. Infra-red rays can't get through our atmosphere, so these telescopes are put into orbit.

Ultra-violet   Extremely hot things give out ultra-violet rays and X-rays. Most of these rays are also blocked by the atmosphere – which is just as well for life on Earth because these rays can harm us.

Young hot stars give out ultra-violet rays. Pulsars give out huge bursts of X-rays.

Radio waves   The coolest things in space give out radio waves. These rays *can* get through the atmosphere, so radio telescopes can be built on Earth. They look nothing like ordinary telescopes. It takes a giant metal dish to pick up radio waves from space. Huge gas clouds give out radio waves.

The Canada–France Hawaii Telescope

How to count the number of visible stars

You can count the number of visible stars by using a bent coat-hanger. Pull the hanger into a square shape and hold it out at arm's length. Move the hanger until it frames the stars in the bottom corner of the sky. Count the stars inside the square. Then keep your eye on a star in the corner of the frame and move the hanger along so that it surrounds the next square of stars. When you have covered the whole sky like this, add all the numbers to get a total.

Constellation spotting

Can you find this constellation? It is called the Plough.

The constellation viewer

You need a square tube (use a cereal packet or a sheet of cardboard) and several sheets of plain paper. Cut the paper into oblongs. The oblongs should be as wide as the tube but they should be longer. Cut out a square window from one of them. Trace the pattern of a constellation onto each of the others and prick the dots with a pin. Now fasten one of the sheets and the frame across the end of the tube, using an elastic band. Finally look through the tube towards a dim light.

The planisphere

The planisphere shows you which stars are overhead at any date and time. The bottom sheet is a map of the stars that can be seen above the Northern Hemisphere. You'll find it on page 47.

Trace the design on this page and cut out the circle. Put it over the star map so that the arrow points to the date. These are the stars that can be seen at midnight on that date.

Now move the arrow along a notch for every hour to get to the right time. (Move it anti-clockwise to get to times before midnight and clockwise to get to later times.) This is to allow for the rotation of the Earth.

Which stars are overhead at midday on your birthday? (You will have to move the pointer round 12 notches to get to midday.) These stars include the constellation of your birth sign.

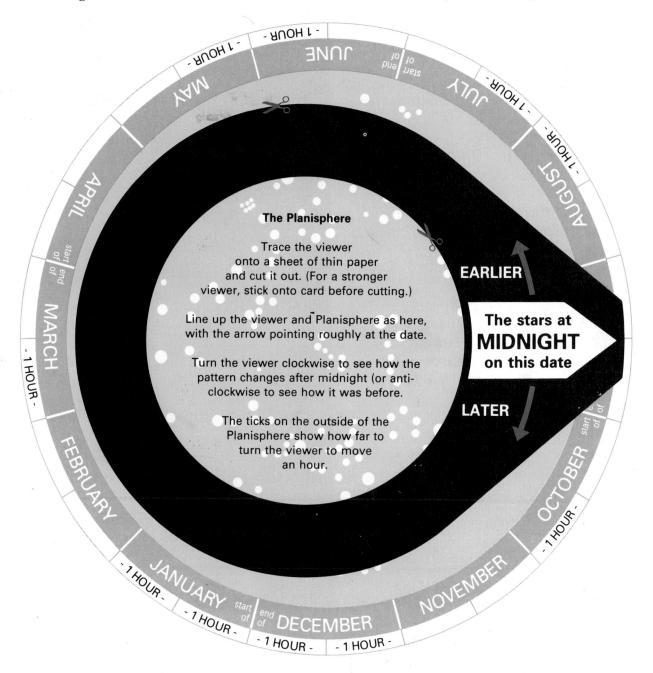

The Planisphere

Trace the viewer onto a sheet of thin paper and cut it out. (For a stronger viewer, stick onto card before cutting.)

Line up the viewer and Planisphere as here, with the arrow pointing roughly at the date.

Turn the viewer clockwise to see how the pattern changes after midnight (or anti-clockwise to see how it was before.

The ticks on the outside of the Planisphere show how far to turn the viewer to move an hour.

EARLIER

The stars at
MIDNIGHT
on this date

LATER

The Universe

The universe is huge but scientists don't think it was always this big. In fact they say if you go back in time far enough, the whole universe of stars and planets and galaxies and gas clouds was crammed into a space no bigger than a pin-head. Imagine telling that to the ancient Egyptians!

The Sun and Earth are about 5 thousand million years old. The universe is three times older. It popped into existence from nowhere as a tiny ball. Suddenly with an enormous bang it exploded. This is called the 'Big Bang' theory.

The dust rushed out in every direction. There were no stars yet – the whole universe was as hot as the middle of a star. Eventually swirls of dust began to gather and inside these swirls the first galaxies were born.

No one can say if this theory is right. After all, no one was there to see it happen! These ideas are based on clues left in the universe today.

Clue 1
The universe still seems to be spreading out. Scientists think it is happening more slowly now. The stars are pulling on each other by the force of gravity and this is gradually slowing them down.

Clue 2
The temperature in space is not as cold as it could be. Scientists think some heat is left over from the time when it was incredibly hot.

The end of the universe
One idea is that the universe will finally stop spreading out and will start flying back together. This is called the Big Crunch theory! Another idea is that it will go on spreading, ever more slowly, but will never quite stop.

The Horsehead Nebula

More questions

What was there before the universe?
What is outside the universe? No one
knows. Even these ideas are not certain.
The universe is the biggest mystery
in space!

Did you know?

- What would happen if you went to the edge
of the universe? If you keep going long enough in
any direction, scientists think you would find
yourself back where you started. (They say it's like
going right around the world.)

Return of the Aliens

The search for alien life

There are many ways to look for aliens. Scientists can send space probes to check the other planets in our solar system. Astronomers use their telescopes to search the skies for other stars with planets. Scientists study the Earth to find out how life began here. Other telescopes are designed to listen for radio signals from alien travellers.

UFOs

Some humans claim that aliens have already visited the Earth. There is a report of a UFO or 'Unidentified Flying Object' just about every day somewhere in the world. Most of these 'Alien Space Craft' turn out to be weather balloons or odd-shaped clouds, or even the planet Venus. That still leaves about 15 UFOs every year which have never been explained.

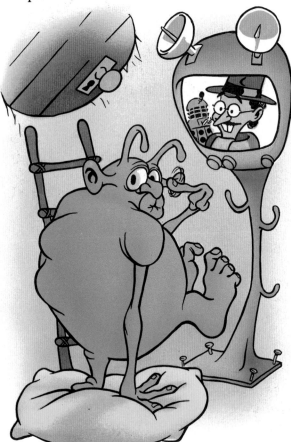

A message to the aliens

Meanwhile we are sending out messages, in case any aliens are looking for signals themselves.

Pioneer 10 has now passed Pluto in its journey out of the solar system. It carries a message board with a picture of a man and a woman, and a map of where the Earth is.

The Voyager space probes are also now heading into space. They are carrying records with the 'sounds of Earth'. These include animal noises, human voices and music.

In 1974, the Arecibo telescope sent out a message in radio waves. It also had a picture of a human, plus details about chemistry, the number of people on Earth and the numbers from one to ten.

In fact, humans have been sending signals into space for the last 60 years. Since the invention of radio and television, we have been bouncing TV signals all around the Earth. Those signals also escape into space. They travel at the speed of light. So perhaps the first clue the aliens will get that humans exist is an episode of 'Dr Who'!

Question

If an alien invited you into its spacecraft, would you get in?

Did you know?
- *Close encounters of the first kind* are when a UFO is seen but doesn't interfere with its surroundings.
- *Close encounters of the second kind* are when the UFO does affect things around it – for example nearby trees catch alight or there are marks left in the ground.
- *Close encounters of the third kind* are when aliens are seen. Often in these cases there are reports of conversations with human beings. Sometimes the human is even invited on board the alien space craft.

The Planisphere

The planisphere shows you which stars are overhead at any date and time. On this page is a map of the stars that can be seen above the Northern Hemisphere. This is the bottom sheet of the planisphere to be used with the arrow heads on the top sheet which you can trace from page 43.

How to assemble your planisphere

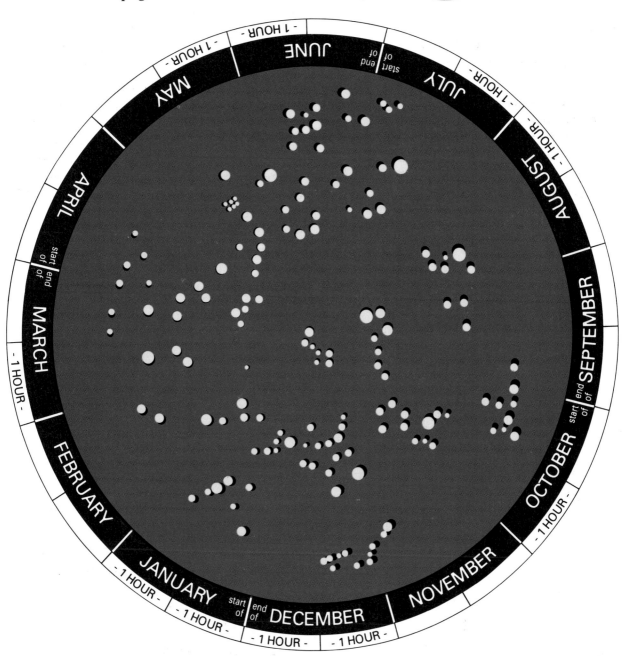

Index

Published by BBC Educational Publishing, a division of BBC Enterprises Ltd, Woodlands, 80 Wood Lane, London W12 0TT

First published 1991
© Berry-Anne Billingsley/BBC Enterprises Ltd 1991

Paperback ISBN: 0 563 34789 9
Hardback ISBN: 0 563 34790 2
Typeset by Ace Filmsetting Ltd, Frome, Somerset
Colour reproduction by Daylight Colour Art, Singapore
Printed and bound by BPCC Hazell Books, Paulton and Aylesbury

Acknowledgements
Picture credits © Genesis Space Library 15, 23, 31; The Granger Collection 8, 40; NASA 4, 13, 14, 20, 27, 30, 32; Ann Ronan Picture Library 6; Royal Observatory, Edinburgh 38, 45; Science Photo Library 19, 37, 41; Telegraph Colour Library 25.

© Illustrations BBC Enterprises Limited 1990
Illustrations © Maltings Partnership 1990, pages 2, 3, 5, 10, 11, 18, 26, 28, 29, 33, 34, 35, 39, 42, 46; Oxford Illustrators 1990, pages 7, 8, 9, 12, 13, 16, 17, 21, 22, 23, 24, 25, 36, 37, 40, 43, 47; Mike Gilkes running head